Science Technology Engineering Math

STEM STARTERS FOR KIDS

ENGINEERING
ACTIVITY
Book

Written by Jenny Jacoby

Designed and illustrated by
Vicky Barker

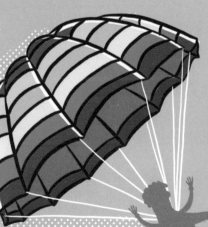

FOR
YOUNG
READERS

WHAT IS ENGINEERING?

Engineering is about finding a problem to solve and finding a way to solve it. Engineers have to pay attention to all sorts of things going on in the world to notice problems they could help with. Then they need to be very creative to find ways of solving those problems. Engineers make things by designing, building and using machines. These machines can be anything from a simple toothbrush (solving the problem of cleaning teeth) to something huge like a wind turbine (solving the problem of finding clean energy).

WHAT IS STEM?

STEM stands for "science, technology, engineering and mathematics." These four areas are closely linked, and engineers couldn't do their jobs without science, technology or math. Math and science are the tools that engineers use to solve problems and create machines. Engineers pay attention to new discoveries in science as inspiration for new tools they can use to solve problems in ways that hadn't been possible before.

Science

Technology

Engineering

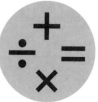
Math

PRINTING PRESS

Back in the Middle Ages, books were hand-written and then copied out (mostly by teams of monks). This meant there were very few copies of books, and each one was very expensive.

The engineer who solved the problem of books being such hard work to make was **Johannes Gutenberg**. His solution was "moveable type"—lots of copies of each letter of the alphabet, made out of metal, which printers could combined in different ways in a printing press to make any number of copies of any text.

Johannes Gutenberg

FACT!

Moveable type was used in Asia for hundreds of years before Gutenberg's invention, but because European alphabets are so much smaller than those in Asia, the invention was even more useful, so it spread very quickly across Europe.

Moveable type goes into a printing press **back-to-front.** This is so it appears the right way round when printed onto paper.

Look at these presses ready for printing—the writing is impossible to read! Use a mirror to see what the text will say when it is printed.

GOLDILOCKS AND THE THREE BEARS

LITTLE RED RIDING HOOD

THE BUILDINGS OF ANCIENT EGYPT

HOW TO BE AN ENGINEER

SPELLS, CHARMS AND POTIONS

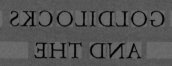

CYCLING ELECTRICITY

What is better than having lights on your bike when it's dark outside? Bike lights that don't need batteries to run! Some bikes have dynamo lights, which are machines that turn movement into electricity. The dynamo fixes to a moving part of the bicycle (the wheel or the hub) and as the wheel goes round, it turns the dynamo and that produces an electrical current. The electrical current gives power to the bicycle light.

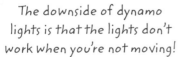
The downside of dynamo lights is that the lights don't work when you're not moving!

It's getting dark but this cyclist's lights are dynamos so she can see where she's going as long as the bicycle is moving. Help her find her way home using the cycle paths and avoiding anything that will make her come off her bike.

7

SEE-SAW LEVERS

Levers are one of the oldest machines in the world, and they help to lift things that would be too heavy to lift by yourself. Levers need something called a "fulcrum" to balance on. By changing the position of the heavy and light things along the lever, heavy things can be lifted more easily.

Something light can help lift something heavy if the heavy thing is close to the fulcrum and the light thing is far from it.

LEVER

FULCRUM

A fun kind of lever is the see-saw.
Heavy and light friends can play
together if they sit in the right places
on the see-saw.

For each of these see-saws, draw the
fulcrum in the place that will help the
see-saw balance.

Remember: to balance, heavy things
need to be close to the fulcrum.

FLYING PLANES

The problem of how to get a large metal airplane, filled with people and luggage, up into the sky and flying seems impossible to solve. One thing that helped engineers to solve this problem is the shape of the wings.

Airplane wings are shaped like an aerofoil. When the plane travels forward quickly (when it speeds up along a runway), the air finds it quicker and easier to move the shorter distance underneath the wing than to travel up over the bump of the wing. With more air underneath the wing, the wing lifts up, taking the airplane with it.

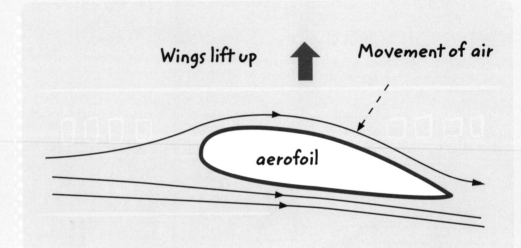

Wings lift up   Movement of air

aerofoil

An engineer who designs planes is called an **aeronautical engineer.**

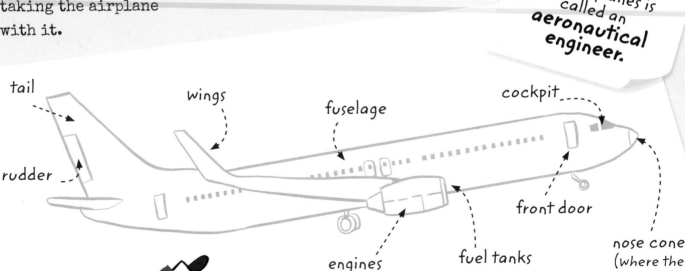

tail

wings

fuselage

cockpit

rudder

front door

engines

fuel tanks

nose cone (where the radar is)

Can you find these aeronautical engineering words in this wordsearch?

```
c  j  o  r  v  i  l  d  j  x  e  s  u  o  h  v  e
x  o  u  a  e  r  o  f  o  i  l  q  g  x  o  r  i
m  o  c  y  i  l  x  v  u  e  l  p  y  z  w  t  h
b  e  s  k  o  k  l  g  c  t  e  k  b  x  i  e  i
u  a  t  o  p  u  b  r  a  d  a  r  d  s  n  u  o
l  n  o  i  t  i  u  b  k  c  e  h  l  i  g  b  t
k  f  z  y  j  l  t  t  j  l  v  e  t  l  u  b  a
h  y  w  i  l  n  u  r  c  d  u  p  l  m  v  u  i
e  c  v  x  t  g  j  e  n  g  i  n  e  a  r  d  l
a  r  s  u  i  o  p  o  k  l  o  v  u  k  m  o  p
d  e  t  u  m  c  u  i  o  p  l  r  u  d  d  e  r
c  y  o  p  u  k  a  n  k  y  k  d  r  x  y  t  m
s  t  j  v  o  b  c  p  z  t  i  j  n  o  k  l  o
d  s  y  i  b  y  f  d  t  l  h  p  o  m  j  l  v
e  y  v  y  r  s  k  u  j  a  m  p  o  c  e  y  m
f  u  s  e  l  a  g  e  v  n  i  o  c  r  i  y  j
m  t  j  v  h  d  o  u  e  u  p  n  v  t  x  u  l
```

aerofoil

bulkhead

captain

cockpit

engine

fuselage

radar

rudder

tail

wing

Answers at the
back of the book.

11

PARACHUTES

Parachutes solve the problem of slowing down a falling person so they can land safely. They do this by increasing the person's air resistance.

When a person jumps out of an airplane gravity pulls them down to earth and air resistance slows them down. A person without a parachute has very little air resistance, and falls very fast. Because parachutes make such a large canopy, they collect a lot of air, and that increases air resistance, which slows the fall—so the person can land safely.

GRAVITY

AIR RESISTANCE

ROLLERCOASTERS

Although rollercoasters throw you up and down hills at thrilling speeds, engineers have worked out how to make the ride go by itself, without the power of an engine. Actually, engines turn on just once in a rollercoaster ride—to pull the rollercoaster up the first hill. After that, natural forces power the ride.

Once the rollercoaster is past the top of the first hill, gravity takes over and pulls the riders the rest of the way.

When the rollercoaster starts going down that first drop, it goes so fast it gathers enough energy to send it all the way up the next hill—and so on, as it whizzes around the whole ride. At the end of the ride, the rollercoaster needs to put on the brakes to get rid of the energy and stop the ride.

The rollercoaster goes downhill faster than it goes uphill. Color in these rollercoaster cars in green if they are going fast, and red if they are going slower.

GLOW STICKS

Glow sticks are great fun for parties but they only last for a few hours. There are three ingredients inside a glow stick and as soon as they mix together it starts to glow. How do engineers solve the problem of the glow sticks glowing before someone is ready to use them? They keep one of the ingredients separate from the others in a small glass tube. When you want to make the stick glow, you snap the tube and shake—this mixes all three ingredients together.

SNAP!

1.

2.

3.

When chemicals mix together and give off light it is called **chemiluminescence**.

An engineer who solves problems with chemistry is called a **chemical engineer**.

(Answers on page 31.)

EARTHQUAKE PROOF

Some parts of the world have lots of earthquakes. Engineers have thought of ways to stop buildings from falling down even when the ground gives them a good shake. The most dangerous thing about an earthquake is falling buildings. People can survive being on quaking ground but they are in danger if a building falls on them. One way to "earthquake-proof" a building is to let it be able to wobble with the quake. The more it can wobble, the less likely it is to fall down and injure people.

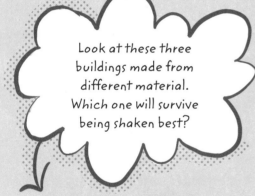

Look at these three buildings made from different material. Which one will survive being shaken best?

Sticks

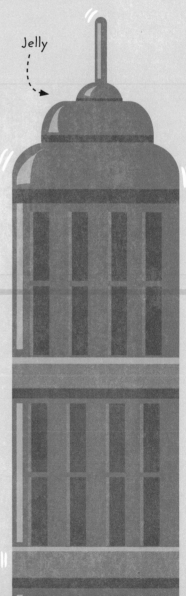

Jelly

Brick

Spot 10 differences between these before and after pictures of an earthquake.

ECO PACKAGING

A problem facing us all is what to do with packaging when we don't need it anymore. Engineers have come up with some clever ways to reduce the amount of packaging we throw away and the amount of trash that builds up on the planet. One way of doing this is by making packaging from reused materials. But the best type of packaging breaks down by itself when you throw it away—this is called biodegradable material. Some packaging even has seeds built into it, so if the packaging is buried the seeds can grow in the ground.

Imagine some packaging for these items. Make sure there is no unnecessary waste and that the materials are recyclable. Draw the packaging on the page.

six eggs

a potted plant

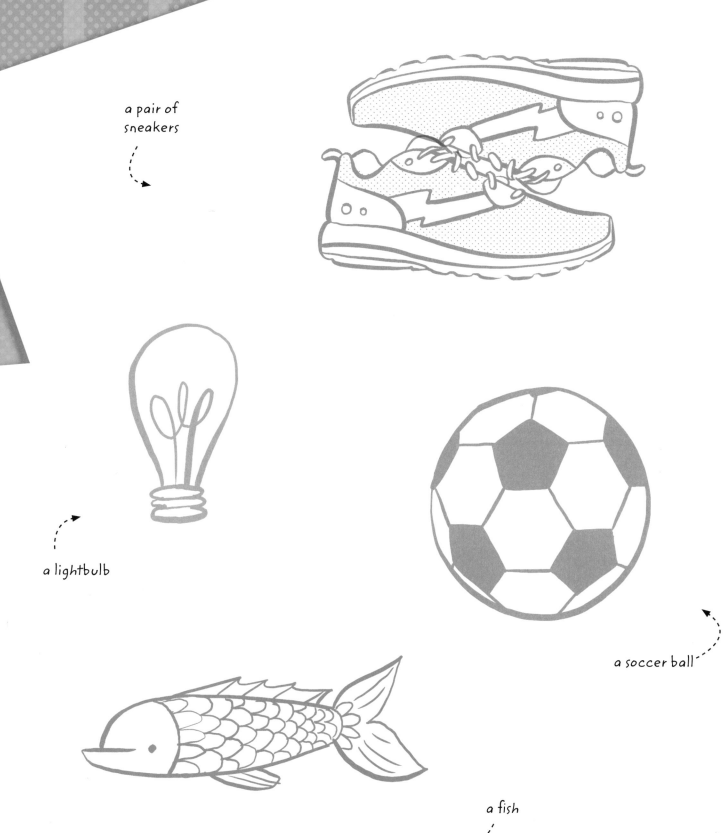

a pair of
sneakers

a lightbulb

a soccer ball

a fish

RUNNING BLADES

Engineers have helped people without lower legs solve the problem of how to walk and run. Running blades don't look like normal legs, ankles and feet but they can make people run just as well as—and maybe even faster than—non-disabled runners. They are made from a very strong but light material called carbon fiber and the way they are shaped makes them bendy like a spring. This springiness helps the runner to sprint forwards in the same way as a natural leg does.

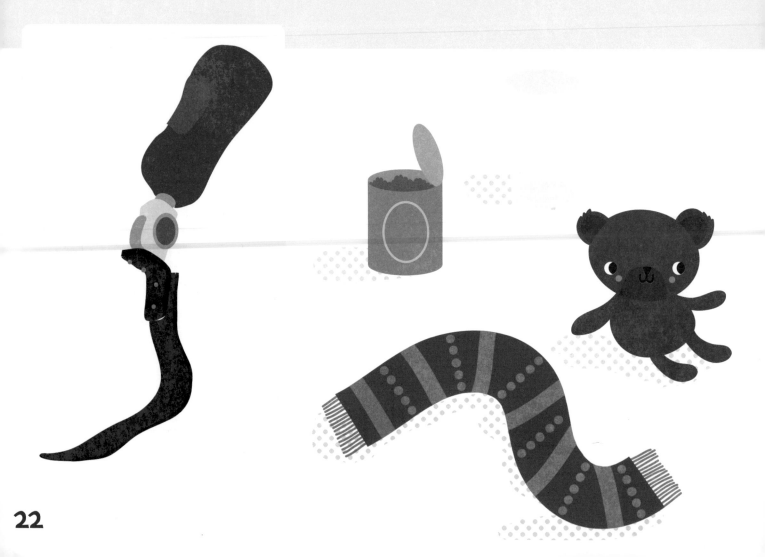

DRONING ON

A drone is a sort of robot that can do its job without a human being there with it. There are drones that work on land and sea but flying drones are becoming more and more popular because they are so useful.

A flying robot with a camera attached to it can get to places and see things that humans cannot—and it can do it more quietly than a human in a helicopter!

Contains a GPS chip to find locations, an altimeter to tell its height, and an ultrasound scanner to tell how close it is to the ground

Controlled by radio waves or Wi-Fi

Four propellers for stability and to carry more

camera

Can you work out which of these jobs a flying drone can do and which are made up? The answers are at the back of the book.

Cook a three-course meal.

Tell farmers which of their crops are not growing properly.

Do your homework.

Help to stop people poaching endangered species.

Help to build a high-rise building.

Put out forest fires.

Shop for clothes.

Help to save lives.

Brush your teeth for you.

Deliver pizza.

Play football.

Film long views from high in the sky for Hollywood films.

Do laundry.

Take selfies.

COMPUTER ENGINEERING

Computer engineers design and build computers to help make our lives easier in a huge number of ways. Computers are part of our everyday lives—not just the computers you write and play on, household devices like washing machines and digital radios have computers inside them as well.

Computers can't think for themselves—they can only do what they are told to do. That means the computer engineers have to do all the thinking first and make sure they give computers the right set of instructions, and in the right order. If there are mistakes in any of the steps, things can go very wrong.

This computer has been given instructions for getting dressed in the morning—but the instructions are in the wrong order! Draw the clothes onto the person opposite in the order the computer suggests. How do they look?

1. Put on shoes.
2. Put on jumper.
3. Put on jeans.
4. Put on T-shirt.
5. Put on underwear.
6. Put on vest.
7. Put on socks.

CODING

Coding is the way of giving instructions to a computer. It's a bit like talking to the computer in its own language. There are two main steps to coding. First, you need to think about the thing you want the computer to do. This could be something like getting dressed in the morning or finding the quickest route to a place. Then you need to break down that thing into a series of instructions. Most importantly, they need to be in the right order, as you saw on the page before.

Think about making a cheese sandwich with six ingredients:

2 slices of bread

mayonnaise

I lettuce leaf

I slice of tomato

I slice of cheese

Tell the computer which order to use the ingredients in.

Can you find these sandwich ingredients in the right order in this set?

ANSWERS

Pages 4-5

Little Red Riding Hood

How to be an Engineer

Spells, Charms and Potions

Goldilocks and the Three Bears

The Buildings of Ancient Egypt

page 7

page 9

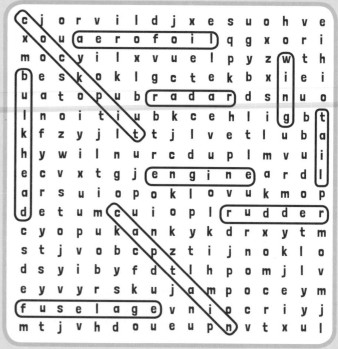

page 11

page 13

page 14-15

page 18-19

The jelly building will survive being shaken best.

page 16-17

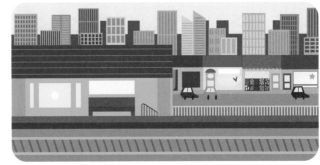

page 22-23

page 25

True answers with some more information:

- **Tell farmers which of their crops are not growing properly.**
  Drones can fly over large areas of farmland to get a better look at how crops are growing, more easily and quickly than a farmer could.
- **Film long views from high in the sky for Hollywood films.**
  Without drones, filming like this would take a lot more equipment and time.
- **Help to build a high-rise building.**
  Drones can carry cables high up buildings and even weave them to help build a structure.
- **Put out wild fires.**
  Drones can fly to spot wildfires and use special cameras to see through fire smoke, giving information to firefighters about the size of the blaze.
- **Help to stop people poaching endangered species.**
  Drones can keep track of groups of endangered animals by flying closer than a human could but keeping enough of a distance to not disturb the animals.
- **Help to save lives.**
  Sometimes drones can deliver life-saving medical equipment faster than an ambulance could get there.
- **Deliver pizza.**
  Drones can sometimes deliver more quickly than someone on a moped, and deliver pizza while it is still hot.
- **Take selfies.**
  With a camera a drone can move to the right place to take a perfect selfie!

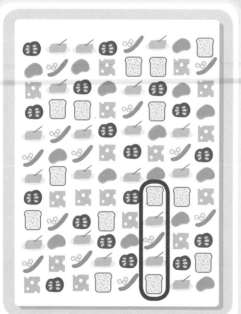

page 29